All of thes ... the book.
Try to match ... ure stickers.

gills wobbeg ... gel shark fin

great white hammerhead whale shark mako

nurse shark cookie-cutter shark *Megalodon* tooth

blue shark squid tail dinosaur pup teeth

killer whale seal pup mermaid's purse stingray

submarine penguins surfboard sea lion friends

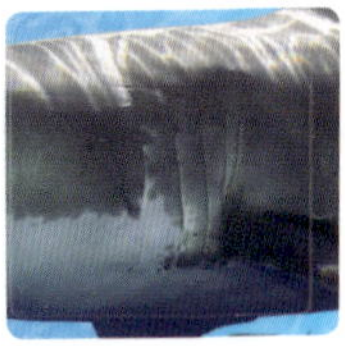
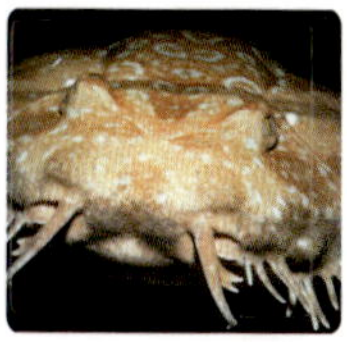

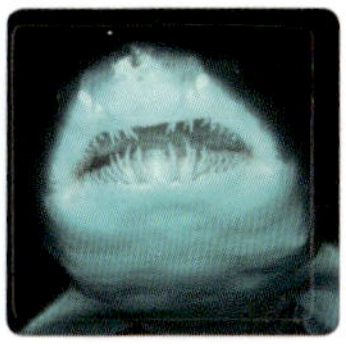

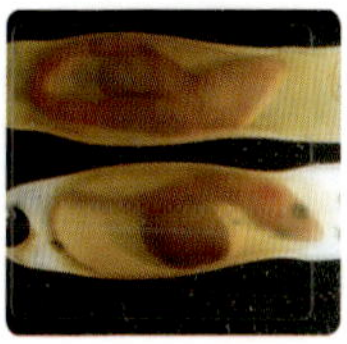

Written by Janine Amos
Reading consultants: Christopher Collier and Alan Howe,
Bath Spa University, UK

This edition published by Parragon in 2011
Parragon
Queen Street House
4 Queen Street
Bath BA1 1HE, UK

ISBN 978-1-4075-1830-5

Printed in China

Sharks

Parragon

Bath • New York • Singapore • Hong Kong • Cologne • Delhi
Melbourne • Amsterdam • Johannesburg • Auckland • Shenzhen

Parents' notes

This book is part of a series of non-fiction books designed to appeal to children learning to read.

Each book has been developed with the help of educational experts.

At the end of each book is a quiz to help your child remember the information and the meanings of some of the words and sentences. There is also a glossary of difficult words relating to the subject matter in the book, and an index.

Contents

What is a shark?

Sharks are fish that live in seas and oceans across the world. Some sharks are tiny, others are giants. Some are gentle and some are fierce.

Sharks don't have bones. Their skeletons are made from light, stretchy cartilage.

Sharks breathe through slits called gills.

There are hundreds of kinds of sharks. Here are just three of them.

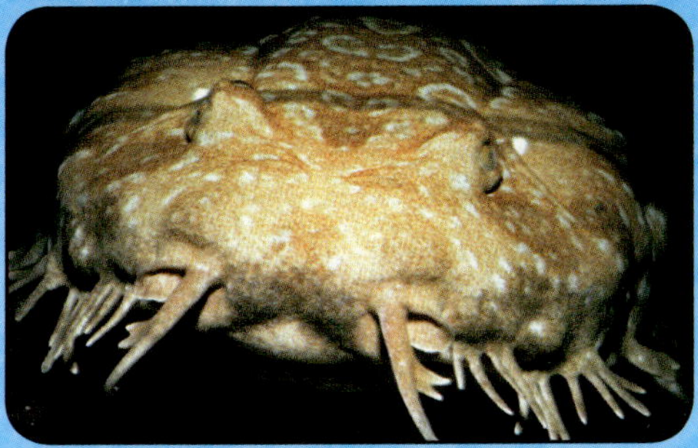

Wobbegongs hide on the seabed. They are well camouflaged.

Dogfish have long, slim bodies to slip through the water.

Angel sharks have flat bodies. They also hide on the seabed.

Amazing!

Sharks have been living on Earth for 400 million years. They were around at the time of the dinosaurs.

Amazing sharks

Can you imagine a fish that has a head shaped like a hammer? Or one that can gobble up a sea lion whole? Sharks are some of the world's most amazing creatures.

The bullet-shaped mako shark is the fastest fish in the ocean. It can swim at over 70 kilometres per hour.

The strange hammerhead shark has eyes on each side of its head. It swings its head from side to side to get an all-round view.

Amazing!

The great white shark eats other sharks for dinner – along with whole penguins, seals and sea lions.

The gentle whale shark is the world's biggest fish. It weighs as much as two elephants.

Swimming

Most sharks are graceful and powerful swimmers. Their smooth bodies are perfect for moving underwater. Sharks swim in S-shaped movements, powered by their tails.

Fins on each side of a shark's body help it steer.

The stiff fin on a shark's back helps with balance.

The shark's long tail beats from side to side, pushing the shark forwards through the water.

Inside most fish is an air-filled swimbladder. It keeps the fish afloat. Sharks don't have swimbladders. Most have to keep swimming or they sink.

Amazing!

The prehistoric shark *Megalodon* may have been up to 20 metres long. Here is one of its huge teeth next to that of a modern shark.

Blue shark

The blue shark is a long-distance traveller. It swims hundreds of kilometres every year, searching for food or to mate.

The blue shark has a bright blue back and a white tummy. These colours help to hide it in the ocean.

Blue sharks hunt with their mouths wide open, trapping fish in the corners. They are slow swimmers but can move very quickly when they attack.

Amazing!

One blue shark made a trip of over 7000 kilometres from New York to Brazil. That's a lot of swimming!

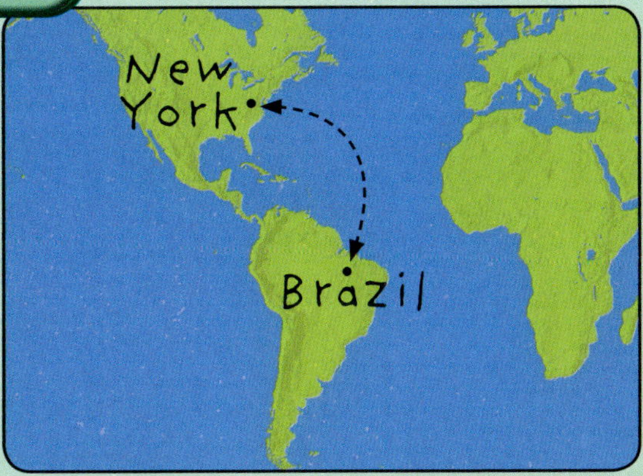

The blue shark feeds on small fish, such as sardines, and on squid (shown left). It lives in warm and cool seas all over the world.

Hunting

Sharks are always seeking out their next meal. They can see, hear, touch and smell, just like people. But their senses are much more powerful.

Touch
A lateral line along their sides helps sharks pick up movements in the water around them.

Hearing
A shark's ears can hear sounds travelling through the water.

Amazing!

An extra sense lets sharks pick up the electric signals given off by fish. This sense is particularly powerful in hammerhead sharks.

Sight
A shark's eyes can see well in dim underwater light.

Smell
Sharks have good noses. They can sniff out blood a kilometre away.

Great white

Great white sharks are giant hunters. They feed on animals such as sea lions and seals, as well as on smaller sharks.

Newborn great whites are already 1.5 metres long. Young sharks eat other fish, such as mackerel and tuna.

Great whites swim near the surface to hunt. But they can dive deeper than a submarine.

Great whites have 3000 teeth. Each one is about as long as your finger.

Amazing!

A killer whale like this, and people, are a great white's only enemies.

Family life

All baby sharks are born from eggs. The eggs of most sharks grow inside their mother. A few kinds of shark lay their eggs on the seabed, safe inside tough egg cases.

Shark babies are called pups.

Amazing!

A blue shark mother can give birth to 50 or more babies at a time.

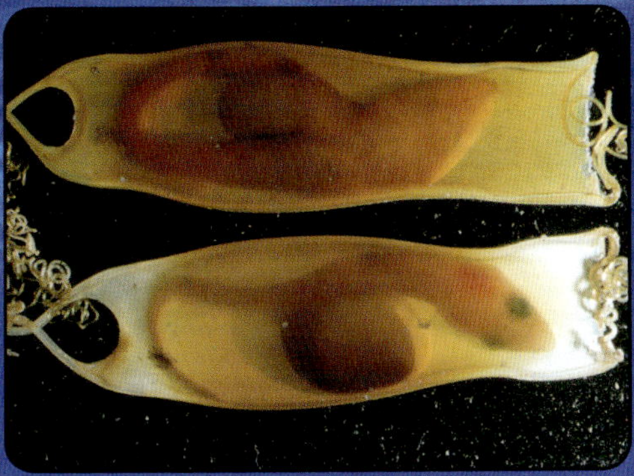

Dogfish eggs are protected by an egg case called a mermaid's purse. The babies grow inside, feeding on the egg yolk.

Lemon shark eggs grow inside their mother. She gives birth to tiny pups, which soon swim off to find food.

Hammerhead

The hammerhead's flat, T-shaped head makes it look different from any other shark. Hammerheads swim together in groups called schools.

Most hammerheads live in warm seas, off the coast of Australia and Central America.

The hammerhead's favourite food is the stingray. It holds the ray down with its 'hammer' and takes a bite.

Amazing!

Baby hammerheads are born with their heads bent backwards, so they don't get stuck inside their mother.

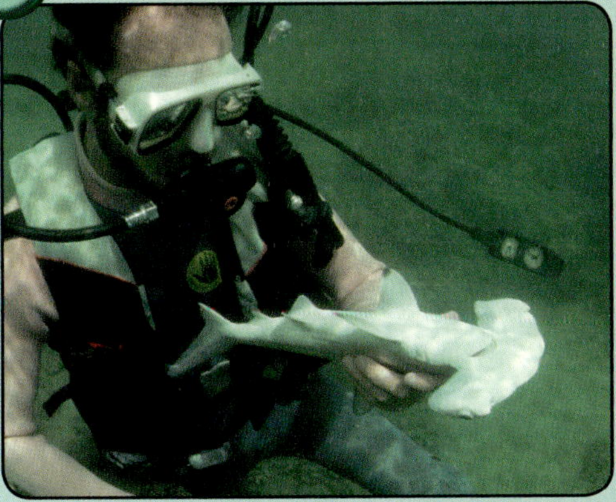

Hammerheads swing their heads from side to side as they swim, picking up smells and sounds in the water.

Their eyes are far apart on their huge heads.

Are sharks dangerous?

Most sharks don't eat people. But some sharks, such as the great white, the bull shark and the tiger shark do attack. There are fewer than 100 attacks every year worldwide.

To stay safe, swim with your friends. Never swim if you are bleeding, because blood attracts sharks.

People are putting sharks in danger. We kill them for food and for sport.

If you see a fin above the water looking like this it means that a shark is near you.

Amazing!

A swimmer on a surfboard can look like a seal – to a shark.

Quiz

Now try this quiz!
All the answers can be found in this book.

How long have sharks been living on Earth?

(a) 40 years
(b) 400 years
(c) 400 million years

Which shark is the fastest fish in the sea?

(a) The mako shark
(b) The great white
(c) The wobbegong

Which parts of a shark's body help it steer?

(a) The fins
(b) The teeth
(c) The gills

What do young great white sharks eat?

(a) Plants
(b) Fish
(c) Penguins

What is a hammerhead shark's favourite food?

(a) Chocolate
(b) Seaweed
(c) Stingrays

What are baby sharks called?

(a) Pups
(b) Fry
(c) Spawn

Glossary

Cartilage	Strong, stretchy material that forms a shark's skeleton.
Fins	The wing-like parts of a fish that help it steer and balance.
Gills	The parts inside a shark's throat that let it breathe in water.
Lateral line	A line of tiny hairs along a shark's body. The lateral line picks up movements in the water.
Mate	To pair up in order to make babies.
Mermaid's purse	The egg case of a dogfish. At first the cases are soft. They soon become hard and will protect the egg.

Prey	The animals that a shark hunts and eats.
Pups	Newborn sharks.
Senses	To see, hear, taste, touch and smell. Sharks have an extra sense for picking up electrical signals from their prey.
Stingray	A type of fish with poisonous spines on its tail. Rays are the cousins of sharks.
Swimbladder	A tiny air-filled bag that helps some fish to float. Sharks don't have swimbladders.
Yolk	The yellow part of an egg that feeds the growing baby shark.

Index